How Many?

A COUNTING BOOK / CHRISTOPHER DANIELSON

STENHOUSE PUBLISHERS
PORTLAND, MAINE

Stenhouse Publishers
www.stenhouse.com

Library of Congress Cataloging-in-Publication Data available.

Book design by Blue Design (Bluedes.com)
Photography by Scott Dorrance (Dorrancestudio.com)
Food Styling by Lorie Dorrance (Loriedorrance.com)

Manufactured in the United States of America

24 23 22 21 20 19 18   9 8 7 6 5 4 3 2 1

This is a book about numbers and counting, but it's different from other counting books.

This book doesn't tell you what to count. It doesn't start with small numbers and end with big ones.

Instead, you decide what to count on each page. You have many choices. The longer you look, the more possibilities you'll notice.

When you're ready to start counting, turn the page.

Look at this picture.
How many do you see?

Ever since 1 April 1960, when Dr. Martens boots first rolled off the production line and onto the feet of postmen, policemen and everyday workers, our reputation for durability has become footwear folklore. Over 100 million pairs later, our belief in making things to last is as strong as it's ever been.

If you thought "How many *what* do
I see?," then you get the idea.

Maybe you'll choose to count the shoes.
There are two of those. Or maybe you'll
count pairs of shoes. There's one of those.

There is one box, but how many shoelaces?
What other numbers do you see? Maybe
you see 20 holes for the laces to go
through (those are eyelets). Or four ends
on the shoelaces (those are aglets).

Maybe you see the yellow stitches,
or something completely different.
What other things can you count?

Ever since 1 April 1960, when Dr. Martens boots first rolled off the production line and onto the feet of postmen, policemen and everyday workers, our reputation for durability has become footwear folklore. Over 100 million pairs later, our belief in making things to last is as strong as it's ever been.

Now how many do you see?

What changed? What stayed the same? What new things can you notice and count?

This book is filled with sets of pictures. Within each set, you'll find many things to count. Some things change. Some things stay the same. Some things might surprise you.

If you're reading this book with friends, tell them about your ideas. Listen to their ideas. See how many things you can find to count together.

Ever since 1 April 1960, when Dr. Martens boots first rolled off the production line and onto the feet of postmen, policemen and everyday workers, our reputation for durability has become footwear folklore. Over 100 million pairs later, our belief in making things to last is as strong as it's ever been.

How many?

How many?

How many?

How many?

How many?

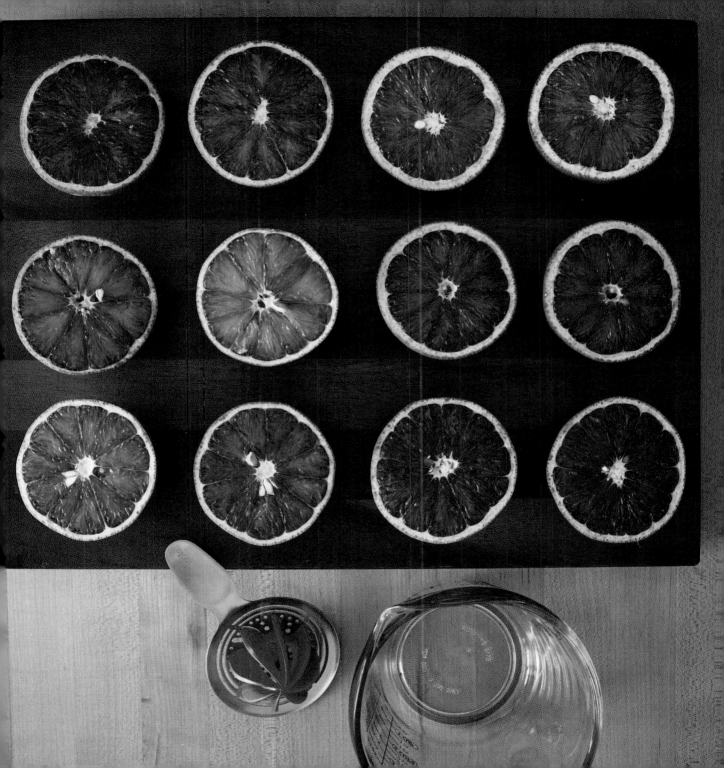

How many?

How many?

How many?

How many?

How many?

How many?

How many?

Once you've read this book a few times, you might think of new questions to wonder about while you read, such as these:

What is the largest number you can find in this book?

What is the smallest number you can find in this book?

What number is most surprising to find in this counting book?

What's your favorite number? Can you find that many of something on one of the pages of this book? Can you find it on every page?

What numbers are missing? (Somebody once told me that there aren't seven of anything in these pictures. Do you agree?)

I made this book to spark conversations, thinking, and wonder.

I hope this is a book you will leave open, think about, and return to often. I hope you will share it with others.

I hope you will find interesting things to count in your world.

I hope you will send me a picture or drawing that has many answers to the question "How Many?"

Find me at talkingmathwithyourkids.com.